OUR WORLD IN COLOUR
KHAJURAHO

OUR WORLD IN COLOUR KHAJURAHO

Photography by
Anthony Cassidy and Pankaj Shah
Text by Shobita Punja

The Guidebook Company Limited

Distributors

Australia and New Zealand: The Book Company,
100 Old Pittwater Road, Brookvale, NSW 2100, Australia.

Canada: Prentice Hall Canada,
1870 Birchmount Road, Scarborough, Ontario MIP 257, Canada.

Hong Kong: China Guides Distribution Services Ltd.,
14 Ground Floor, Lower Kai Yuen Lane, North Point, Hong Kong.

India and Nepal: UBS Publishers' Distributors Ltd.,
5 Ansari Road, Post Box 7015, New Delhi 110 002, India.

Singapore and Malaysia: MPH Distributors (S) PTE Ltd.,
601 Sims Drive, No. 03/07-21, Pan-I Complex, Singapore 1438.

USA: Publishers Group West Inc.,
4065 Hollis, Emeryville, CA 94608, USA.

Photography by **Anthony Cassidy** 6, 10-11, 14(top, middle), 15(top), 16, 17, 18 (top), 20(top),21, 25, 26, 32-33, 34, 39, 42, 43, 49, 50, 51 (top left), 52(top, bottom right), 53, 55, 57 (bottom right), 58(top),61, 62-63, 64, 66(bottom left & middle), 69 (right),71 (top left), 72, 73, 80.
Pankaj Shah 2-3, 5, 7, 8-9, 14(bottom), 15 (middle, bottom), 18 (bottom), 19, 20 (bottom), 22-23, 24, 27, 28-29, 30, 31, 35, 36, 37, 38, 40-41, 46, 47 48, 51 (top right, bottom left and right), 52 (bottom left), 54, 56-57, 60, 66 (top, bottom right), 67, 68, 69(left), 70, 71 (top right, bottom), 75 (right), 76, 77, 78, 79; also **Toby Sinclair** 44-45, 58(bottom), 59, 65, 74-75

Text and captions by Shobita Punja
Edited by Nick Wallwork
The author and photographer would like to thank the Hotel Chandela and the Taj Group of Hotels for their assistance in the production of this book.

Printed in Hong Kong

ISBN 962-217-129-X

Title spread
The Kandariya Mahadev temple is the best known of the temples at Khajuraho. It stands 36.5m(116 ft) above the ground set on a high plinth. The temple consists of four chambers each with their own roof; the first, an entrance porch, leading to a hall and then the great hall (maha mandap), before reaching the sanctum (garbha griha) which is positioned exactly below the towering Sikhara. This temple is dedicated to Siva and the shrine now has a marble lingam or phallic symbol of the creative power of the deity.

Right
The Kandariya Mahadev temple is the largest and arguably the most architecturally perfect of all the temples at Khajuraho.

Pages 8 & 9
The Sivsagar or Sibsagar tank beside the Western group of temples forms an important part of village life and temple ritual. Pilgrims and local inhabitants bathe here before entering the temples for prayer. The early rulers of Central India realised that the wealth of their kingdoms lay in appropriate water management and constructed huge tanks throughout the area.

The quality of locally quarried sandstone lent itself perfectly to intricate carving and delicate workmanship. The colour of the stone varies from a pale buff to brown and reflects the changing moods of the sun and moon. The light plays on the planes and contours of the wall, casting deep shadows to contrast with areas that are in direct sunlight.

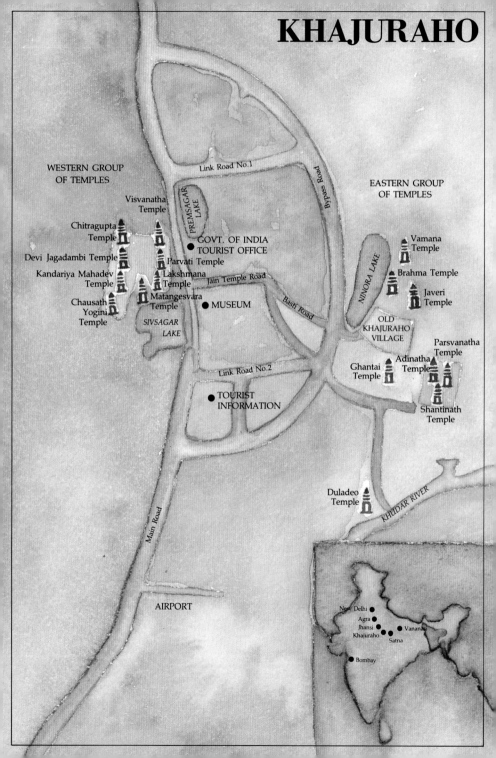

INTRODUCTION

KHAJURAHO WAS, for many centuries, a small obscure village in Central India; then in 1839 a British army engineer, Captain I S Burt, visited the area and rediscovered an extraordinary group of temples built in the eleventh and twelfth centuries.

Since then, programmes for restoration and research have brought Khajuraho back into the limelight. Once again the world can admire the creative genius of India's builders, the beauty of her temples and the sensuous charm of her sculptures.

Khajuraho is situated in Madhya Pradesh, south of the Gangetic Plain and north of the rising Deccan plateau. The expansive landscape of the state is cradled by the Vindhya and Satpura hill ranges and watered by large rivers, the Narmada and Chambal. The wealth of forests in the region has sustained animal and human life for centuries and in the wildlife parks at Panna and Bandavgarh one can still appreciate how the beauty of nature inspired the poets and artists of the land.

Nature's bounty also provided the builders of Khajuraho with excellent building material from the marble rock gorges of the Narmada and the sandstone valley of the Ken River. There are also rich deposits of iron, copper and tin in the area, and diamond mines in Panna, which have aroused the avarice of many rulers through the ages. Owing to its strategic central position, Madhya Pradesh played an important role in Indian history. Evidence of habitation from the Stone Age onwards has been found in cave paintings around Bhopal, the state capital. As time went by, traders, migrants and pilgrims brought new religions and ideas to this region and Sanchi, near Bhopal, became a major centre of Buddhist pilgrimage in the second century BC. The monumental buildings and fine sculptural decorations of Buddhist art at Sanchi influenced generations of artists in the region. Hindu art and architecture also evolved in Madhya Pradesh from the small humble shrines at Sanchi and Deogarh to the soaring heights of the temples of Khajuraho.

History of Khajuraho

Myths, legends, ancient literature and inscriptions provide a jigsaw–puzzle picture of the story of Khajuraho, but there are still some missing pieces. There is mention of Khajuraho in ancient texts which explain how the village got its name. *Jejabhukti* is one derivative name, and *Khajurapura* means 'the village (*pura*) with golden date palms (*khajura*)'.

The *Mahaba Kand of the Primal Raso*, a folk ballad of the seventeenth century, recounts a beautiful legend concerning the origins of the Chandella dynasty, who came to rule the region in the tenth century. There was once a young princess called Hemavati whose sublime beauty attracted the attention of the moon god, Chandra. One night, as she was bathing by the river, Chandra appeared in the guise of a young man and made love to the beautiful princess. From their happy union a child was born, blessed by the gods. He was brave and fearless, and among his exploits it is told that he slayed a lion without any weapon. This heroic figure is believed to have founded the Chandella kingdom. Their emblem is of a young man grappling with a lion, and at Khajuraho there are a number of sculptures of this scene.

The story of the moon god and the princess is rather fanciful, but not unusual. It was customary, especially in north India, for rulers to trace their descent from either the sun (*surya*) or the moon (*chandra*) to sanctify their power and authority. With the creation of this legend to bolster their lineage, the Chandellas, a group of minor chieftains, grew to become powerful rulers between the tenth and twelfth centuries with their capital at Khajuraho and forts at Ajaygarh, Mahoba and Kalinjar.

Inscriptions on the walls of the temples at Khajuraho provide information on the genealogy of the kings, their military achievements and the temples that were built

The temples are adorned with sculptures; images of gods like Siva's elephant–headed son Ganesh (top), *figures of women and couples in various poses* (centre) *and mythical creatures that ward off evil and protect the gods, temples and devotees* (bottom).

during their reign. The Chandella ruler Harsadeva of the tenth century was succeeded by his son Ysorvarman or Lakshavarman (c. AD925—950) who expanded the kingdom and is said to have built the Lakshmana temple at Khajuraho. Dhanga (c. AD950—1002), the next ruler, waged war with his neighbours and brought new areas under his control. According to the inscriptions, he was responsible for building the Visvanatha temple and providing his patronage to merchants and followers of the Jain religion who settled in his territory. Under Ganda (c. AD1002—1017) and Vidyadhara (c. AD1017—1029) the Chandella kingdom expanded and several more temples were added to their capital in Khajuraho. It was during their reign that the monumental temples of Devi Jagadambi and Kandariya Mahadev were built, and that the threat of invasion from Islamic rulers in the north was first felt. Subsequently, their lands fell under the sway of the Sultans of Delhi and the name of the Chandellas became submerged in history.

The 14th century traveller Iban Batutah, an Arab from North America, describes in his chronicles a place called Kajarra with large temples that had been mutilated by the iconoclasts, and ponds and lands beside which Hindu sages and teachers practised asceticism and discussed philosophy.

Today, Khajuraho remains a village with only a few thousand inhabitants who grow wheat and vegetables on small plots of land and graze their cattle and goats on the dry pastures and hillsides. The village houses are still white-washed mud huts with tiled roofs and children playing outside in the streets. With the influx of visitors, an airport was opened a few years ago and luxury hotels have sprung up in and around the village. Except for a few shops and traders selling fake antiques, erotic postcards, slides and books, the peace and tranquility of the village has remained, as yet, undisturbed.

The layout of Khajuraho is quite simple. A road links the airport to the centre of the village. At the entrance to Khajuraho there is a large welcome sign and beside it the Sivsagar tank, said to have been constructed for the benefit of travellers and pilgrims by Jain merchants almost a thousand years ago. There is a belief that there were as many as 80 temples built in and around Khajuraho of which only 20 exist today in fairly good repair. The temples seem to have been constructed in clusters which, for purposes of identification, have been termed as the Western and Eastern groups according to their location. There are several other temples scattered around the village and interesting mounds which, for lack of funds, have not yet been excavated. Further research in Khajuraho may reveal a more complete picture of the capital of the Chandella rulers and explain the location of the temples within the plan of their city.

The most important temples, belonging to the Western Group, are situated beside the Sivsagar tank on the main road. They are enclosed within a garden maintained by the Archaeological Survey of India. The well-laid lawns, trees and flowerbeds around the temples, which are recent embellishments of the site, provide areas of viewing, photography and relaxation without the obstructions that usually surround temples under worship. To the left of the entrance gate is the Lakshmana temple, in front of which is a small open pavilion called the Varaha temple. Beside this on the northern side is the only living temple dedicated to Matangesvara or Siva, the conqueror of death. To the right of the entrance is the Visvanatha temple, in front of which is the Nandi pavilion. At the other end of the garden rises the great Kandariya Mahadev temple, the Devi Jagadambi and, to the northern side, the small Chitragupta or Sun temple.

A comfortable twenty-minute walk or ten-minute rickshaw ride leads to the Eastern Group of temples. Within this complex of Jain temples under worship are the Parsvanatha and Adinatha temples of the Chandella period. Close by, to the south-west, is the Duladeo Jagadambi and at the same distance on the way to the airport, the Chaturbhuj temple.

Opposite the Western Group of temples on the central village road is the Archaeological Museum of Khajuraho which houses a fine collection of sculptures salvaged from the ruined temples. Across the road, for lack of funds and space, is a repository for damaged images which have been lying in the open for almost a century.

The Temples: Concept and Design

The temples of Khajuraho represent the culmination of the Central Indian style of architecture which evolved over centuries of experimentation. A Hindu temple is built to sanctify a holy place or to shelter an object of veneration. The site where a temple is built holds some significance for believers, and there is usually a local myth or legend narrating how the gods visited the place and what they did there. The priest who serves at Matangesvara temple narrates a beautiful legend of the origin of the 2.5 m (eight foot) gigantic *linga* image of his temple. The myth is centred on the marriage beween Siva and Parvati, two important deities of the Hindu pantheon. Siva, the Creator-Destroyer of the universe, was an ascetic dressed in animal skins and smeared in ash, lost in meditation, without a thought of marriage and physical love. The other gods were keen to get him married and ensure the birth of a son who would protect the world. They found an appropriate goddess, Parvati, to be his bride, but Siva would not be disturbed. The gods then sought the help of Kama, the Indian god of love, who with his arrows found a chink in Siva's contemplative armour. Furious that his meditation had been disturbed, Siva opened his third eye and reduced the god of love to ashes. To show his power and strength a great *linga* or phallic image of Siva appeared, and this of course, is the image at Khajuraho. Siva and Parvati then get married and the god of love is restored.

Once the holiness of the image and sanctity of the place was established, the construction of the temple could begin. As worship grew in popularity and royal patronage was extended to the shrine, early bamboo and brick structures were replaced by stone buildings. A temple had to be built in accordance to the rules given in religious texts like the *Silpa Shastra*, and throughout the length and breadth of India these rules are still followed faithfully. According to the text, the temple symbolises the universe and must be built to face the four cardinal directions, in alignment with the position of the planets, stars and sun. For this reason most of the temples at Khajuraho face the rising sun, so that the first rays of light fall on the entrance to the shrine.

A temple is also likened to the Universal Being and the body of the temple, like the human body, has several interrelated parts, a metaphor similar to the western medieval concept of a church. The most sacred part of the temple is a small room, the *gargha griha*, housing the idol—the womb and creative centre of the building. The room is dark, calm and silent like the soul and centre of the universe. Only the initiated are allowed to enter this sanctum, and if this area is defiled, the entire temple loses its purpose of being.

The sanctum is sheathed in walls of brick or stone like the outer manifestation of the body. Representations of the gods in their appropriate postures facing the cardinal directions are fixed on to the outward facing walls. These sculptures protect the temple and guide the devotee from the transient world of existence to the stable quiet centre within the temple and within the mind and soul.

The devotee is required to walk around the temple, following a clockwise direction, once, thrice, or seven times, in a symbolic circumambulation of the universe, before entering the temple. The temples at Khajuraho have been built on high platforms with broad bases for *pradakshina* or the processional walk around the temple. Some of the temples such as the Lakshmana, Visvanatha and Kandariya Mahadev temples have narrow passages around the sanctum within the building as well for similar purposes.

The walls of the temples acquire a rippling effect with projecting and receding areas that are decorated with bands of sculptures, patterned mouldings and punctuated with niches and balconies.

The surface of the outer walls of the temples is bound together by two or three bands of sculpture, creating a perfect balance of verticals and horizontals.

The body of the temple rises from the platform and its vertical towers pierce the sky, as though fixing the position of the heavens in relation to the earth. The roof tower built over the sanctum is called the *sikhara* and by its shape and height, acquires the most prominence in the building. The contour and form of the sikhara is distinct in each style of architecture in India. At Khajuraho it is tall, elegant and curvilinear in shape, and often made up of miniature replicas of itself. The roofs of the halls in front of the shrine are pyramid–shaped with diminishing horizontal tiers. Each roof ends with a circular, ribbed cushion-like member, on which is placed the *kalasa* or pot, symbolising ambrosia, the nectar of immortality and plenty.

The larger temples of Khajuraho resemble in profile a mountain range, with each component of the roof–tower rising towards the highest point. The mighty Himalayan mountains, the majesty and lofty purity of their snow-clad peaks, were believed to be the home of the gods. It was this imagery that the artists strove to recapture when they built these temples.

The plans of the temples at Khajuraho range from single-roomed shrines with small porticoes to ones with several halls and passages. The large temples like Kandariya Mahadev have ground plans in the form of a double cross. In this design the entrance of the temple is at one end of the cross which opens into a long hall with the sanctum at the opposite end. Branching out from the hall are four projections which end in balconies that provide ventilation and light. These projections of the cross create an outer wall surface that is not straight but almost star-shaped, with angles and turns that play with light, casting shadowy ripples along the temple walls.

The temples at Khajuraho, when seen from a distance, have a strong vertical character with all parts assembled as if straining towards the sky. As one gets closer, one finds that the entire wall of the temple is divided into distinct horizontal bands of mouldings and sculptured panels. A perfect sense of balance and equilibrium has been created by this symphony of vertical and horizontal planes.

The walls of the temple unfold in a never-ending wave of projections and recesses that follow the plan of the building, the horizontal bands seeming to bind the building together in a complex integrated scheme. Bold rows of architectural mouldings begin at the base of the temple and project out of the wall. Above the base, the wall space is divided into horizontal bands of varying sizes: some temples have two, three or four narrow horizontal bands with scenes and figures, followed by two or three broad bands half a metre (two feet) or more high of figurative sculptures on the main body of the temple. The bands are divided and separated by decorative scrolls, creepers and stencil-like patterns. The monotony of the wall plane is broken at intervals by a projecting balcony with squat pillars, sloping sides and roof, and overhanging eaves. A dramatic entrance to the temple is provided by a flight of stairs that raises the temple level high above the platform.

To build the temple, huge blocks of granite for some of the earlier temples and bases, and sandstone from the banks of the nearby Ken River were hewn and transported to the site. Hundreds of thousands of artisans over several generations worked together to create these temples, which have a remarkable homogeneity in style, workmanship and quality of artistic skill. Master artists must have overseen the work of the others, bringing a touch of genius to individual sculptures and a sense of unity and balance to the entire scheme of sculptures in one temple.

After consultation of horoscopes and signs—the initial rituals for the foundation of the temple—the actual building work would have begun. In Hindu architecture little or no use was made of mortar or cement, as the pre-cut stone blocks were joined by intricate interlocking hinges and metal clamps. Sculptured figures were also cut before being fixed into allotted spaces. This technique required careful planning beforehand and meticulous supervision. This method was used for two associated reasons; stone could not be carved *in situ* while on the building, in case of damage, and a damaged image was considered inauspicious. Therefore, individual figures were first carved out of single blocks of stone, while sculptured panels were divided into units which were then fixed together in sequence.

The quality of sculpture rests to a great extent on the nature of the material, and at Khajuraho the sandstone of the region is superior. Sandstone is a sedimentary rock created from layers of sand deposits; for this reason the colour of the stone in the temples at Khajuraho varies enormously from building to building, from pale buff to yellow, pinkish yellow and biscuit brown. The stone also reflects light in different ways, changing each day and each season with the intesity of sunlight and the glow of moonlight. Sandstone also has a softness that was used to great advantage by the skilled artisans of Khajuraho in depicting the female form—the curve of the hip, the swell of the breast, the subtle contours and cheek and chin, the fleeting quiver of a smile.

Extensive restoration work on the temples has contributed to preserving the freshness and ageless quality of the sculptures; the stone too has weathered well, despite the erosion of time, wind and rain.

Images, Figures and Sculptural Themes

The sculptural adornment of the temples at Khajuraho has been classified into five types: (1) *Geometric and floral motifs,* to be found on panels, architectural mouldings and pillars, and intricate ceiling designs that unfold like lacy flowers and stars from the roofs within the temple halls. (2) *Panels depicting scenes from court life,* religious stories, hunting scenes, music and dance and processions. (3) *Mythical and realistic animal figures,* generally placed at intervals along the broad bands of the exterior temple walls to break the monotony of figurative forms. Some elephant sculptures on the base mouldings of the temple (as in Lakshmana temple) are depicted as though they were supporting the building on their backs. (4) *Images of gods and goddesses,* usually installed in the niches below the balcony projections at the back of the temple, and sometimes incorporated into the broad bands of sculpture. The most important sculpture in the temple was the idol installed in the main sanctum. (5) There are countless depictions of *amorous couples and female figures* that constitute the main subject of the broad sculptured bands on the body of the temple. These figures are also to be found within the temple, the walls of the hall, circumambulatory passages, brackets and ceilings.

The bands of sculpture on the outer wall are up to two–and–a–half feet high. They lose none of their sensuous or aesthetic quality when seen individually or as part of the scheme of wall decoration.

The carved forms follow the rules laid down in the *Shastras* specifying the size and proportion of each part of the body and the postures, gestures and iconographic details that should be used. The artists in Khajuraho worked within the prescribed framework and yet gave to the sculptures a quality and style of their own. At Khajuraho the portrayal of the human body is frank and sensuous. The arms and legs have been elongated slightly to make the limbs elegant and expressive. The senuousness of the figures is created by the languid posture of the body, the curl of the fingers and the inclination of the head. The eyes are long and tapering—as suggested in poetry, like lotus buds—the nose straight, or hooked like a parrot's beak, the lips serious or in a smile, rarely showing the teeth. The stone figures seem to pulsate with life as they are always shown in movement, whether subtle or vigorous. The best sculptures are to be found in the Lakshmana, Visvanatha and Kandariya Mahadev temples, while a certain grossness and heaviness is apparent in the sculptures at the Parsvanatha temple and the later Chaturbhuj temple (though in style and execution they are similar).

Sculptors throughout India never over-dressed their images. The figures were depicted draped in the finest textiles, meant not to conceal but to accentuate the beauty of the human form—breasts, hips, torso and limbs. In Indian art the human body was always depicted without embarrassment, with a pride and pleasure in the aesthetics

The temple interiors are also profusely decorated with sculptures, ornamental pillars, brackets, doorways and patterned ceilings.

of physical form, be it male or female. The warmth of the Indian climate and a belief that unstitched cloth was pure, led to a minimal style of clothing. Jewellery for the hair, ears, nose, neck, waist, arms and legs was elaborate, the variety of designs of earrings and necklaces worn by the ladies of Khajuraho is quite impressive. Yet the jewellery is never excessive; its function is suggestive—to draw the eye to the turn of the ankle, the firm contours of the breast and the soft cheeks of the face.

Erotic Sculptures and Female Figures

In all Indian temples there are depictions of animals, geometric patterns, narrative scenes and images of gods and goddesses. However, nowhere else is there such a profusion of female figures, couples and lovers on the main body of the temple walls. Several theories have been offered to explain why the artists of Khajuraho decorated their temples in this manner.

The first reaction to the sculptures of lovers and almost naked female figures came from British officers whose Victorian sentiments were deeply offended. They held the view that Khajuraho represented the decadent phase of Indian culture. Alexander Cunningham who surveyed the site in 1862 describes the sculptures as 'indelicate', 'disgustingly obscene', as the female figures were 'purposely exposing their persons'. Others felt that the explicit scenes of love-making and the rather acrobatic sexual positions were a form of teaching, a way to train people in the art of love as specified in the famous *Karma Sutra* texts. Some opinions that the depiction of lovers and erotic art was believed to ward off evil spirits and protect temples from lightning and disaster. Others are of the view that the erotic art stems from an esoteric Tantric cult that incorporated sexual activities as part of their rituals. Dr Devangana Desai, a leading art historian, suggests that Indian erotic sculptures are visual representations of religious texts. Since a large number of the erotic sculptures are on the broad bands of the outer wall, and are located at the junction where the shrine room meets with the hall room, that passage of interralation has been translated into a visual pun—the 'joining' of couples. Stella Kramrisch, a noted American art historian, interprets the female figure as the symbol of the human soul, waiting, yearning and preparing herself to meet God. She is often shown lingering, looking at her reflection in a mirror, touching her breast, stretching herself as if to awaken her soul. The couples in union, embracing and discovering each other, suggest the central Hindu principle of the re-integration of the wholeness and harmony.

Yet none of these theories explain why all the temples depict figures of women engaged in specific activities like washing their hair, looking in the mirror, painting their feet, applying kohl to their eyes, why most of the women have their backs half-turned to the viewer, or why there are repeated figures of Siva and the other gods with their wives. This author feels that perhaps the temples at Khajuraho were designed to celebrate a particularly auspicious event, the marriage of Siva and Parvati.

The marriage is described in religious and secular literature in great detail. The legend narrates how Siva was persuaded to get married by the arrows of love, and how he finally came to the wedding with all the gods and goddessess. When he arrived at the city, all the women and inhabitants were busy in their household activities, bathing, dressing, 'entertaining' their husbands, applying make-up or playing with their children. When they heard Siva's marriage procession they turned away from whatever they were doing to behold their handsome lord. What the artists at Khajuraho have captured is that single dramatic moment when human beings become aware of the presence of god, an everlasting moment of universal joy and wonder.

Western Group of Temples at Khajuraho

This complex consists of the five most important temples in Khajuraho.

Lakshmana Temple

The Lakshmana temple is one of the earliest in the group and is attributed to King Yasovaram, also called Lakshavarman (c. AD925—50). It is built upon a three metre (nine feet) broad platform, with the main temple occupying the centre and four subsidiary shrines at the corners. Along the platform is a row of sculptures with scenes from daily life, religious myths and processions of horses, elephants and warriors. The exterior wall of the main temple has two broad bands of sculptures of gods, female figures and couples. This temple has the finest examples of Khajuraho's sculptural art.

The entrance is by an imposing flight of steps, decorated at the top by an elaborately carved stone arch. The pillared hall leads to the sanctum, whose doorway is rich with carvings and bands of sculptures of lions, cherubs, incarnations to save the world from disaster (as fish, a tortoise, a boar, a half-man-half-lion, and as various heroes), Rama of the epic poem Ramayana, Krishna the cowherd or divine lover, and others. Images of these incarnations are to be seen here and at other temples.

Varaha Temple

This is a small open pavilion-type temple facing the Lakshmana temple. The roof of the pavilion is pyramid–shaped, made up of diminishing horizontal tiers similar to the smaller roofs of the main temple. The shrine rises high up on a three metre (ten feet) plinth and contains a large—2.5m by1.5m (8ft 9in by 5 ft 10in)—monolithic image of Varaha the boar, the incarnation of Vishnu who saved the earth from primeval floods. The image is of highly polished sandstone and decorated with more than 600 figures of gods and goddesses in neat rows.

Mantangesvara Temple

This temple stands on a high platform, approached by a dramatic flight of steps. It stands adjacent to the Lakshmana temple, and from its simple pyramid–shaped roof a huge flag of Siva sways in the breeze to proclaim that it is still under worship. The sanctum hall is only 1.5m sq (25ft sq) and contains three balcony windows. The sanctum hall is supported by massive walls and interior pillars. In the centre is a huge pedestal from which rises a *linga* that is 2.5m (8 ft) high and more than one metre (3 ft) in diameter. The *linga* is a phallic symbol representing the creative power of Siva. The colossal sculpture is of polished sandstone and has several inscriptions on its surface.

These designs, developed over centuries of experimentation, synthesise motifs from both Buddhist and earlier Hindu architecture. At Khajuraho they are perfected and create a sense of movement that harmonises with the static solidity and bold profile of the temples.

Visvanatha Temple

In plan and form, the Visvanatha temple resembles the Kandariya Mahadev and Lakshmana temples. However, it is built on a high platform which it shares with the Nandi temple. The main temple stands in the centre of the platform, with two extant shrines of the original four subsidiary shrines at the corners. From the platform terrace one gets a good view of the temple wall mouldings and the images in the outer niches, and of the three broad bands of sculptured figures. Within the temple, the main hall and passageway around the shrine contain some of the loveliest sculptures of Khajuraho, which cling to every nook and corner of the wall. The pillars of the hall once carried several ornamental carved brackets, of which only a few exquisite examples remain. The ceiling of this temple is also extraordinary with carved designs of many-petalled flowers and hanging stamens. Around the doorway of the sanctum is an elaborate frame of bands of sculptures. Within the shrine is a small stone lingam (this temple is dedicated to Siva), and in the porch is a stone slab inscription stating that King Dhangadeva (c. AD 950-1002), who built the temple, had installed a stone and emerald lingam — which has, of course, disappeared. It is believed that the offering of an emerald or jewelled lingam indicated the fulfilment of a wish. Dhangadeva lived to the ripe old age of a hundred and achieved his wish in the expansion of the Chandella empire from Gwalior to Vidisa and from Varanasi to the Narmada.

Nandi Temple

This open pavilion which faces the Visvanatha temple resembles the Varaha temple and has a huge pyramid–shaped roof. The roof is supported by a series of pillars resting on a low wall. The colossal polished monolithic image of Nandi, the faithful mount of Siva, is placed facing his lord and master within the main temple. The gentle bull is seated in a very naturalistic manner, with his tail curled by his side.

Kandariya Mahadev Temple

This has been acclaimed as the most magnificent temple of Khajuraho. It stands on a long platform that is shared by a small porched shrine with the Devi Jagadambi temple on its right. The platform is three metres (10 ft) high and the towering *sikhara*, rising to a height of 30.5m (102 ft) is almost as long as it is high. *Kandariya* denotes 'Siva-who-dwells-in-a-mountain-cave', and the pyramid–shaped hall roofs and sikhara are meant to signify the proverbial mountain of Kailash in the Himalayas. The sikhara is made up of a series of smaller replicas of itself that cluster and rise upward to form this awe–inspiring stone edifice.

The exterior temple wall is divided into bold architectural mouldings and three broad bands of figurative sculptures. The erotic sculptures are clustered into two areas on the north and south side, in the juncture between the shrine and main hall.

There are three representations on each side of the couples in rather acrobatic union being watched or assisted by attendants. The human groups are divided by vertical bands carved with *naginis* or snake goddesses, figures and mythical animals.

The temple is approached by a flight of stairs and has a beautiful ornate stone archway of four loops with miniature figures in movement incorporated in a decorative design. Within the hall here are eight pillars with brackets. The elaborate doorway leading to the sanctum has several scrolls with mythical animals and nymphs, and at the base are figures of the purifying river goddesses Ganga and Yamuan. Within the sanctum is a marble *lingam*.

Devi Jagadambi Temple

On the same platform as the Kandariya Mahadev temple, dedicated to Siva, is the smaller temple of Devi Jagadambi now assigned to the goddess Devi, Siva's consort. Between the two temples is a sculpture of a rampant lion and a warrior, the emblem of the Chandella rulers. The temple has a long porch, vestibule and shrine. The carvings on the outer wall of the temple are especially beautiful. The elegant elongated figures of women undressing and anointing themselves, lovers in impassioned embrace and deities are classic examples of the sculptures of Khajuraho.

Chitragupta Temple

This temple stands a little distance away, to the right of the Devi Jagadambi temple, and has the same plan, as it was built in the same period.

The Chitragupta temple was originally dedicated to Surya, the sun god. Inside the temple shrine is an image of Surya, shown riding his chariot of the sun driven by seven horses. The seven horses represent the seven colours of the rainbow, or days of the week. Lotuses are also essential to the iconography of Surya, since they open and blossom as the sun rises each day.

The Buddhist, Jain and Hindu sculptures found at Khajuraho have distinct aesthetic qualities reflecting the philosophies to which they belong.

The Eastern Group

This complex of temples consists of several Jain temples of a later period that are still under worship. Within the courtyard are the Parsvanatha and Adinatha temples that for a long time were classified as Jain temples of the Chandella period. However, though the images inside the *garbha griha* are now of Jain origin, the entire scheme of the temple seems to indicate that they were originally Hindu temples.

Jainism, a breakaway sect of Hinduism, was founded some time in the sixth century BC by Mahavir who, like the Buddha, became an ascetic and preached a simple and moderate way of life. *Ahimsa* (non-violence) and respect for all living creatures is an important injunction of this religion. Many wealthy merchants were converted to the new faith, attracted by its advocacy of social equality, as against the Hindu caste system that placed merchants lower in the social hierarchy than Brahmins and Kashatriyas, the warrior/ruler caste. Even today, wealthy merchant communities belong to this faith and have built shrines and pilrimage centres in Rajasthan, Gujarat, Orissa and Karnataka. Here in Khajuraho, the Jain merchants built their shrines from the tenth to eleventh centuries, under the patronage of Hindu rulers.

The sandstone sculptures have remained in remarkably good condition despite centuries of exposure to the harsh climate.

Parsvanatha Temple

This is the largest temple in this group and has a slightly different ground plan from the others. The sculptures on the outer wall are similar to those on the main group of Hindu temples, as this temple was originally Hindu. Some of the figures playing musical instruments or adorning themselves with ankle bells, clothes and make-up are noteworthy. Within the shrine are the images that have been installed later of seated *tirthankaras*, the succession of 24 holy teachers of Jainism, of whom Mahavir, the founder of the faith, was one. These images seem almost rigid and lifeless in comparison with the sculptures that adorn the outer walls of the temple.

Beside the Parsvanatha temple is the Adinath temple which again has a slightly different design. Unlike the *sikhara* of the other temples of Khajuraho, the roof of this temple is not made up of layers of mini-*sikharas*, but has a tall, conical roof, with beautiful lattice-work patterns of *chaitya* windows along its sides.

There are very few sculptures of lovers on this temple. The topmost band on the exterior wall is smaller than the lower two and carries figures of *apsaras* (sky nymphs) and attendants carrying garlands and musical instruments.

The Museum at Khajuraho

The Khajuraho Archaeological Site Museum has a fine collection of sculptures retrieved from the temples. The galleries of the museum have been classified according to the theme of the sculptures: the Siva Gallery, Vaishnava Gallery, the Jain sculptures and another gallery of assorted panels, figures and brackets.

In the entrance hall stands a colossal sculpture of a dancing Ganesh, the charming elephant-headed son of Siva, who is worshipped at the begining of all Hindu rituals as the remover of obstacles and the bringer of prosperity and good fortune. In the Vaishnava gallery there are several sculptures of the different incarnations of Vishnu. The Bhu-Varaha is the incarnation of Vishnu as a giant boar who saved the earth from primeval floods. The earth is personified as a gentle goddess lifted up by the boar. Another beautiful image is of the Lakshmi Narayana pair, though it is badly damaged (only a fragment of the torsoes and heads remains), Vishnu or Narayana and his consort Lakshmi, the goddess of wealth, hold each other in loving embrace—the artist's tribute to the never-ending story of love that is celebrated throughout the temples of Khajuraho.

(Right) *The lion attacking a warrior commemorates the legendary founder of the Chandella dynasty, who as a young man defended himself barehanded against the animal's attack. There are several images like this in and around the temples, and it is considered the emblem of the Chandellas.*

(Below) *Inscriptions carved on pillars, walls and stone slabs now reset in the porch walls of some temples are often in verse, eulogising the temple patrons and Chandella kings, providing historians with interesting information. The language used is often Sanskrit, the mother of many modern Indian languages, and the script is Devnagari, which is still used today.*

The temples of Khajuraho are famous for their architectural perfection and infamous for their erotic sculpture.

(Following pages) Thought to have been built by the Chandella rulers of Central India in the tenth to twelfth centuries, the temples had long been abandoned and surrounded by thick jungle. When rediscovered by Captain Burt in 1838 he remarked that they are 'most probably the finest aggregate number of temples congregated in one place to be met with in all India, and are within a stone's throw of each other'.

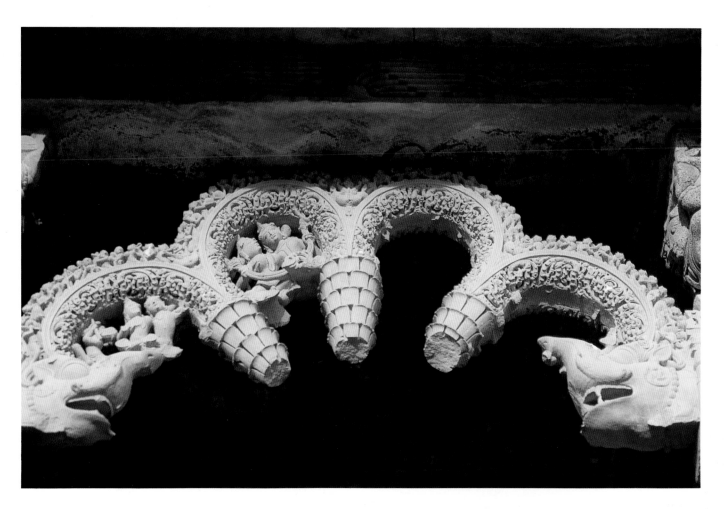

The Kandariya Mahadev temple takes its name from Siva who 'resides in a mountain cave'. Facing east and the rising sun, the frontal perspective of the temple entrance is dark and cave-like. The ornamental gateway is made of a single stone, intricately carved into four loops, representing a garland, that rests on the heads of mythical crocodiles.

Left

In the inscriptions the temple towers are compared with 'snowy peaks of the Himalayas' like Mount Kailash where Siva is said to reside. The towering sikhara *is made up of miniature replicas of the same design that cling and rise on the surface of the tower as though each is yearning to reach the sky.*

The architectural mouldings at the base of the temple (above) provide the transition between the platform and the body of the temple. The sandstone base is carved in bold geometric designs resembling traditional jewellery. Between the mouldings are narrow friezes with musicians, dancers and processions celebrating the arrival of the gods.

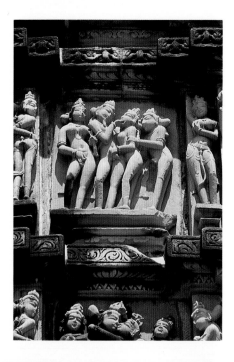

Sir Alexander Cunningham, whose contribution to Indian archaeology is phenomenal, counted 872 statues on this temple in his 1864 report, of which 646 were on the outside walls. Between the balconies of the north and south side of the temple are the 'erotic sculptures'. Several theories have been put forward to explain why such scenes adorn a temple. Are they an interpretation of the **Karma Sutra**, the ancient Indian treatise on love and lovemaking, or part of some esoteric Tantric ritual?

The female figures that flank the gods on the temple walls are always in movement although they appear to stand still. The artist has captured a moment when the women are engrossed in a variety of activities; taking off their clothes, playing with a ball, stretching or painting the soles of her feet.

Following pages
The Devi Jagadambi temple and the small pavilion-like Mahadev shrine dedicated to Siva share the same plinth as the Kandariya Mahadev temple.

The Devi temple is distinguished by the excellent quality of statuary on the outside walls. These sculptures, placed above eye–level, have been carved with such precision as to correct the viewer's perspective. The figures of the gods are depicted standing in a relaxed pose and can be identified by the symbols and weapons that they hold, while the female figures are engaged in a variety of activities.

(Left) *The double–cross plan of the Lakshmana temple, with balconies such as these on the south side, provide light and ventilation to the inner chambers. They are an architectural element that provide a variation to the wall scheme and by extending the walls provided the artists with more space. The distinctive conical* sikhara *above the shrine contrasts pleasingly with the layered pyramidal design of the* mandap's *roof.*

(Above) *The door frame to the main shrine is decorated with a number of auspicious symbols; most important amongst them are the female personifications of the two major rivers of India—the Ganga and the Yumana. These are always placed at the base of the frame and are shown either carrying a pot, standing beside their attendants and/or standing on their* vahanas *(celestial vehicles)— the crocodile and turtle respectively. According to Hindu belief, bathing in these two rivers can wash away all sins and the statues are therefore positioned at the temple door to purify all who enter.*

In the sanctum of the Devi temple is the image of Devi Jagadambi, which seems to have been placed there at a later date, because the original lintel above the doorway indicates that this temple was probably dedicated to Vishnu.

'For when one is with a mate, one is whole and complete.' Stella Kramrisch, an eminent American art historian, explains the embracing couples as a symbol of moksha, the reunion of spirit and nature, the ultimate goal of every being.

(Left) There are several endearing sculptures of lovers that convey their passion and desire, echoing contemporary Sanskrit love poetry which likens the embrace of lovers to a vine entwined around a tree.

(Above) Some of the friezes provide an insight into the actual building of the temples and the labour involved as well as contemporary life.

(Right) The Chaturbhuj temple.

The Lakshmana temple is the only one to
have a walled plinth with small subsidiary shrines on the four corners. The
temple is dedicated to Vishnu. To the left
of the temple is the Matangesvara temple
which houses a huge 2.5m (eight feet)
polished lingam, this remains a popular
place of worship.

The Lakshmana temple (above and right) is one of the earliest of the Western Group and has survived superbly the ravages of time and human abuse.

Right
As a visitor undertakes the ritual clockwise circuit or pra-dakshina of the temple, the profile of the building changes dramatically with each new perspective.

(Left) The Eastern Group consists of old, reconstructed and new temples, some of which are still used for worship.

(Below) The Reneh Falls, approximately 19km (11 miles) west of Khajuraho on the Ken River. The sandstone found by the river was used to build many of the temples.

Statues of the gods are distinguished by their elaborate and often peaked hairstyles and crowns (above), while the attendant figures wear an assortment of fashions and hairstyles. As it is the Hindu custom to wear unstitched clothes (considered to be pure) both men and women are seen with fine fabrics incorporating elegant designs, held at the waist by delicate belts and chains (left). The Indian climate and sensibility towards nature created an attitude of honest pride with the human form and there was no necessity to obscure the beauty of it.

It is possible that the artists may have been familiar with the Karma Sutra; an ancient text which describes the art of love, the preparation of the body, anointing oneself and one's partner, the art of kissing, love bites, seduction, the use of the hands and various postures and positions. Hindu philosophy acknowledges four integrated and essential aspects of life; one of these, Karma, is the physical fulfillment of life which is as important as the spiritual and intellectual.

The large female figures standing beside these gods are usually shown in one of a number of poses, some of which are repeated. Exceptionally finely carved, they evoke an air of sensuousness with the twist and turn of the body and the fineness of detail.

(Right) In both secular and religious architecture the doorway or entrance is perhaps one of the most important elements of a building. The artist endeavours to decorate it in stone as a householder would with natural flowers and leaves.

The frieze along the plinth of the Lakshmana temple depicts a series of scenes that may have once told a story but now seems to be jumbled in the restoration of the temple. There are court scenes, a young dancer performing before a king, musicians,

processions of elephants and horses, warriors carrying a variety of weapons and more erotica. The Lakshmana temple is the only one with such a frieze around its plinth.

The mouldings at the base of the Lakshmana temple are perhaps the most elaborate. Bas relief and 'stencil–cut' designs are interspaced with a frieze of elephants that seem to support the weight of the temple. Even in such minute detail the artist gave character, humour and expression to each figure; the elephants and attendants each reflect a different mood.

The monolithic image of Varaha (below), the boar incarnation of Vishnu, is elaborately carved with over 600 figures of gods and goddesses in neat rows. It is customary to place in front of a temple a small pavilion which enshrines the main animal personification of the temple deity. (Left) In front of a Siva temple the seated nandi, *or bull, on which the God rides. The building diagonally in front of the Lakshmana temple is an open pavilion, with a pyramid–shaped roof, that contains a 2.6m (eight foot)–long standing monolithic figure of Varaha, the boar incarnation of Vishnu (below). Varaha is said to have rescued the earth, personified as a goddess from the primeval floods represented here by the water-serpent at his feet.*

Opposite page
As the sun sets on Lakshmana temple, the figures become bathed in the golden evening light, and the lengthening shadows seem to bring them to life.

At the base of the steps leading to the actively worshipped Matang-esvara temple is a delightful figure of the seated Ganesh, the lord who removes obstacles. Worship consists of evoking the five elements that constitute nature: water, fire, ether, air and earth represented by holy water, lamps, incense, bells and flowers.

(Right) The sun sets behind the Visvanatha temple. In March each year Madhya Pradesh Tourism organises a week–long festival of dance with the Visvanatha temple as a backdrop.

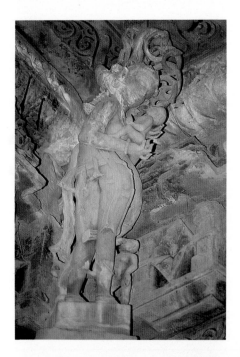

The Kandariya Mahadev, the Laksh-mana and Visvanatha temples all have a circumbalatory passage around the inner sanctum lit by the balconies (left). The soft, diffused light that enters the inner chamber illuminates the exquisite sculpture surrounding the shrine. The sculpture on these inner walls is often far superior to that on the outside.

The inner halls are supported by sturdy pillars with ornate capitals and sculptured brackets. The bracket figures of women are among the finest sculptures at Khajuraho but unfortunately many have been stolen or destroyed.

Scholars have speculated on the number of years it may have taken to build each temple. The stonecutters most probably assembled the temple with finished blocks of sculptured stone and then moved them into their alloted place and position.

(Above) *The Visvanatha temple dedicated to Siva once had four minor shrines placed on the platform, of which only two remain.*

(Right) *A shrine with a large image of Hanuman, worshipped as the loyal monkey companion of Rama in the epic of the Ramayana. This image bears an inscription that dates it as one of the earliest at Khajuraho. The image is covered in a paste of turmeric, vermillion and ghee.*

The Visvanatha temple, like the Kandariya Mahadev, is also dedicated to Siva and follows a similar plan. Visvanatha means 'Lord of the Universe'. In profile, it is possible to see the evolution of temple design from a single–room shrine to one that incorporates graded entrance halls each with their own roof surmounted by Kalasa, symbolic pot of amrit, the elixir of life that rests on a ribbed, cushion-shaped circular amalaka.

(Opposite top) *Conservation and preservation of the temples is a continuous activity of the Archaeological Survey of India. The Vamana temple stands near the Ninora tank and is a compact structure with a simple plan and exquisite sculpture.*

(Opposite bottom) *Cattle still cross the ford on the Khudar River near the Duladeo temple each evening as they return to the safety of the village.*

(Below and right) *The temples at Khajuraho are lit at night during the winter months. Each year in March a dance festival is organised by Madhya Pradesh Tourism.*

(Following pages)
While the village of Khajuraho is small by Indian standards, itinerant craftsmen visit to provide essential services, to mend tools and sell their wares. Almost 30,000 pilgrims and tourists visit Khajuraho each year without destroying its essential character.

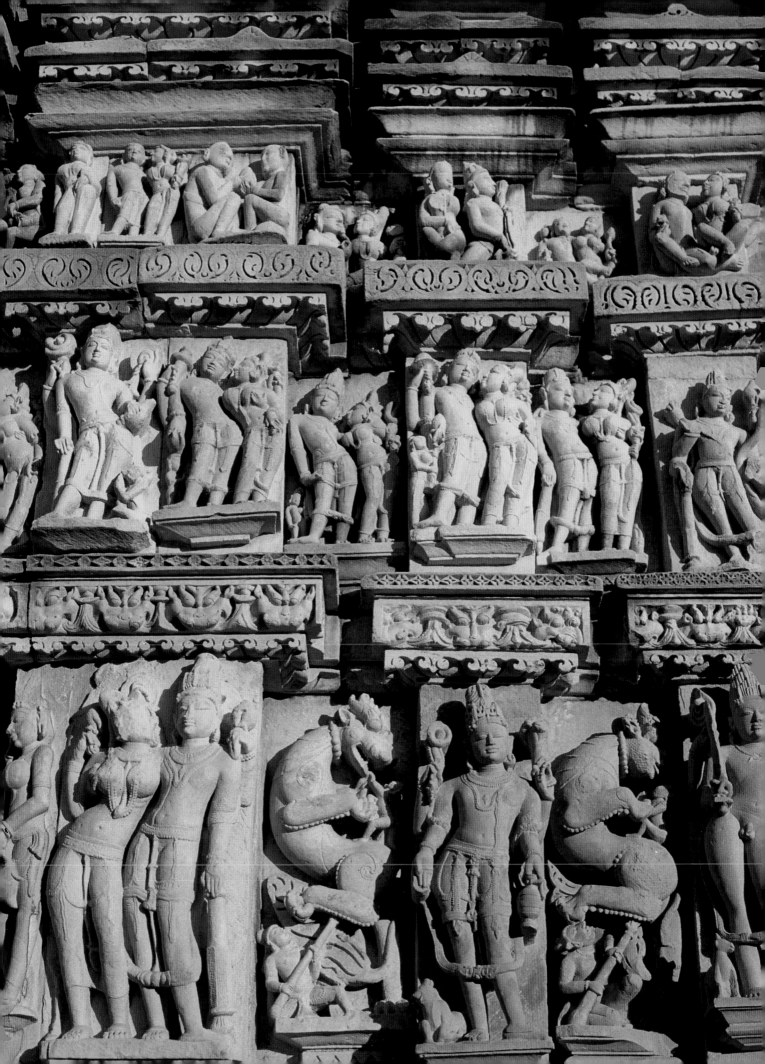

A small service industry has sprung up in Khajuraho to cater to the thousands of tourists who visit each year. These include everything from reproduction antiques (above) to refreshing drinks (left)!

Right
The Vamana temple is dedicated to Vamana, the dwarf incarnation of Vishnu. Standing alone, the temple is notable for the simple design of its shikara.

(Above) *The Parsvanatha temple sits majestically amid the spectacular Western Group of temples and features some classic sculptures, such as the woman removing a thorn from her foot (far left).*

66

There appears to be a sculptural theme at the Parsvanatha temple focused on deities with their consorts who they hold in a firm embrace. There are several sculptures that are common to the temples in the Western Group (left), such as the lady painting her foot (right), the lady applying kohl (top), the lady with mangoes feeding her child (above), and graceful figures of women applying make-up, jewellery and clothing.

(Opposite) *The Hindu pantheon of gods gives equal status to male and female deities. They are often combined with their respective characteristics and attributes to symbolise unity and wholeness.*

Clockwise from top left: *Brahma with Brahmi; Vishnu with Lakshmi; Ram with Sita; and Kama with Rati.*

(Above) *At Khajuraho, the Hindu trinity of Brahma the creator, Vishnu the preserver and Siva the destroyer are often placed together on lintels of doorways and the walls of the temples, to represent the eternal cycle of creation, growth and transformation. Their female aspects compliment and support the gods. Here, Siva holding a trident and snake, stands beside his consort Parvati who holds a mirror, while above are smaller seated figures of Brahma and Vishnu.*

(Above right) *Vishnu, shown here, holds his symbols—the conch (which echoes the sound of creation) and the disk of destruction; while his consort has a mirror in her hand which is ignored as she gazes at her partner's face.*

The Eastern Group of Temples, one mile beyond the village, consists of two temples contemporary to the Western Group and other newer shrines constructed with lintels, pillars and sculptures from older temples. Of the two important temples in the Eastern Group the Parsvanatha temple has a simpler, more solid plan and structure than those of the Western Group (far right) and seems to have been modified and reconstructed in later years. The outer wall decoration consists of three bands. The upper narrow one of flying figures, with the two lower ones of couples, deities with their consorts and mythical animals (above and right).

(Left) *The lion and the warrior, the symbol of the Chandella Dynasty, is a recurring theme at Khajuraho.*

(Far left and below) *The Adinatha temple is perhaps the most ignored of the major temples but in fact has some of the finest sculptures. The female figures here, in contrast with those on the neighbouring Parsvanatha temple, are lithe, slim, sensuous and well proportioned. Unfortunately much of the temple has been renovated and most of the front has been reconstructed.*

The distinctive western wall of the
Duladeo temple is superbly balanced
with numerous deities and attendants.
(Left) The two main figures are a seated
Surya, the sun god, and below, the
broken torso of what must once have
been a splendid figure of Nataraj, Siva in
the cosmic dance of creation.

(Left) *The Duladeo temple, beside a ford on the Khudar Nullah, stands separate from, and south of, the Eastern Group. According to local legend the temple acquired its name from* dhulan *meaning bridegroom, to commemorate the death of a young man who died here on the way to his marriage.*

Although heavily restored and renovated by the Archaeological Survey of India, the temple retains its original character. Similar in plan to the other temples, its distinctive features are the shape of the roof and the intricate flow of its outer wall and inner hall. The main temple wall has two main bands of sculpture surmounted by a narrow band of flying sky nymphs, or apsaras *(above and right) and musicians heralding the presence of the gods below.*

(Left) *The Chaturbhuj temple is the southernmost surviving temple and crowns a small ridge east of the airport. It is unusual in design as it faces west and consists of a single shrine with an enlarged open porch and no mandap.* (Right) *While the lintel indicates this temple was dedicated to Vishnu, with Brahma and Siva beside him, the image within has been identified as a 2.7m (nine foot)–high monolithic statue of Dakshinamurti Siva. The artist's skill in creating the elaborate jewellery, the headdress and the youthful stance make this an exceptional piece of sculpture.*

AN A TO Z OF FACTS AND FIGURES

A

Architecture Architecturally, it is difficult to classify Indian temple- or Hindu art into geographical or stylistic divisions; temples belonging to one period have often borrowed elements from other parts of the country. References in literature mention three broad categories or styles: the *Nagara* (northern, central with an eastern branch), *Dravida* (southern) and *Vesara* (central and western regions). The temples of Khajuraho represent an advanced stage of development of the central variant of the north Indian style of temple architecture.

B

Brahma The Brahma temple on the left bank of the Ninora tank in Khajuraho has a simple plan with a raised platform and pyramid–shaped tower. It is considered to be one of the earliest temples built at Khajuraho along with the Chausath Yogini, Lalguan Mahadev and Varaha temples. The sanctum houses a large *chaturmukha* (four-faced) Siva-lingam with each face showing a different expression representing various aspects of the god, from benign to terrifying.

C

Chaunsath Yogini The Chaunsath Yogini temple at Khajuraho stands south of the Kandariya Mahadev temple, on the banks of the Sivsagar tank. This temple is the oldest at Khajuraho and dates back to the ninth century. The temple consists of small shrines, several of them ruined, dedicated to the 64 *yoginis* or manifestations of Sakti—the goddess of fertility, growth and prosperity.

D

Devi Devi is a general term for the female goddess of the Hindu pantheon. The goddess has several forms and manifestations for she represents life, creation, death and destruction. In sculpture the goddess is depicted either alone in her benign or terrible manifestation, or as consort to one of the gods. The figures of gods with their consorts is a popular theme in Indian sculpture.

E

Eastern Group The Eastern Group of monuments at Khajuraho include three Hindu temples—the Brahma, Vamana, and Javeri. Within the Jain temple complex some of the later temples are still under worship along with the Ghantai, Adinatha and Parsvanatha temples. These temples are of Hindu origin but were later converted into Jain shrines.

Elephants Elephants have been a popular motif in Indian sculpture from Buddhist times. Elephants were tamed and used by royalty in the medieval period and were considered an emblem of status and power, strength and stability. There are several depictions of elephants in processions and in combat in the sculptures of Khajuraho.

G

Ghantai Temple Ghantai temple is situated south-east of the village of Khajuraho, not far from the Eastern Group of Jain temples. This temple has been dated to the tenth century and consists of a hall with several carved pillars. The name of the temple, *Ghantai* (bell), derived from the carved bells motif found on the pillars.

Ganga Ganga is the name of the most venerated holy river in India. It flows from the northern Himalayas through the northern plains of India to the east where it meets the Bay of Bengal. In mythology, the River Ganga was brought down from the heavens to wash away the ashes of the illustrious dead. The force of the descent of the Ganges was broken by Siva, who caught the mighty river on his head. As the waters lost their way in his matted locks they fell to earth as gentle subdued streams. There are other myths that explain the sanctity of the river and for this reason to bathe in her waters, to cremate the dead on her banks and to immerse the ashes at places like Rishikesh, Hardwar and Varanasi is considered auspicious. The goddess Ganga along with Yamuna or Jamuna (an important tributary) are personified in sculpture and placed at the base of the doorway to the inner sanctum of the temple to symbolise purity and the washing away of sins.

H

Hanuman Hanuman is the faithful monkey chief who offers assistance to Rama in the story of the Ramayana. Hanuman helps Rama find his kidnapped wife Sita and together they bring her back safely from Lanka. At Khajuraho there are several primitive shrines dedicated to Hanuman who is worshipped for his strength, loyalty and honour.

I

Indra Indra, the Lord of the Sky, was an important ancient Vedic God until he was superceded by others in the medieval period. Indra can be identified in sculptures and paintings by his *vahana* or mount, a large white elephant called Airavat, who travels through the sky like a cloud.

J

Javari Temple Javari temple is one of the smaller temples dedicated to Vishnu and is situated north–east of the village of Khajuraho, near the Vamana and Brahma temples. The temple faces east, like many others at Khajuraho and has a sanctum, a *mandap* and a porch. The entrance to the porch has an ornately–carved stone *torana* similar to the ones found on the Lakshmana and Kandariya Mahadev temples. The walls of the temple are profusely carved with bands of sculptured figures, flying *apsaras*, mythical animals and amorous couples.

K

Kartikeya Kartikeya is the warrior son–god of Siva and Parvati. He is known also as Skanda, Kumara and Subrahmanya in southern India. The *vahana* or mount of Kartikeya is a peacock on which he rides to battle.

L

Lalguan Mahadev Temple Lalguan Mahadev temple is a tenth century shrine at Khajuraho. The temple is built on an outcrop of granite, faces west and is situated half–a–mile west of the Chausath Yogini temple. Like the Brahma temple it has a simple plan with few ornaments and sculptures.

M

Museums There are several museums with collections of Chandella art salvaged from the temples at Khajuraho. The best collection can be found at the Archaeological Survey Museum at Khajuraho itself. The Indian Museum in Calcutta also has several outstanding sculptures including *Woman writing a love letter*, *Woman playing with her child* and the *avatar* of Vishnu—Bhuvaraha. The National Museum in New Delhi now has a small collection of beautiful specimens of Chandella art including *Lakshmi Narayana* and *Woman playing with a ball*.

N

Naga *Naga* or *Nagadeva* are the sacred serpent gods that rule the underworld and represent the life-giving waters and all the treasures derived from the earth. Worship of snakes is common in many parts of India, especially amongst agricultural communities. They are said to bring prosperity, marriage and offspring to their devotees. The *naga* (male) or *nagini* (female) are depicted in sculpture or paintings as snakes. Siva adorns himself not with jewellery but his companion snakes. Nagas are often represented with human heads and serpent hoods, or with snake-like human bodies.

O

Orcha Orcha lies 11 km (seven miles) south of Jhansi, beside the Betwa River. The rulers of Orcha State built a small city, citadel, palaces and chatris there in the sixteenth century. The Jahangir Mandir and Darbar hall have tilework and painted details of great beauty.

P

Prathiharas Prathiharas were rulers of north–western India with their capital at Kanauj. The Chandella chiefs were local feudatories of the Prathiharas before they established their independent kingdom in the tenth century.

R

Rastrakutar The Rastrakutar were powerful rulers of western India in the ninth century who threatened the kingdom of the Prathiharas. Harsha, the Chandella prince, assisted his Prathihara overlord Mahipala and reinstated him on the throne of Kanauj after the Rastrakutar invasion circa AD917. The Rastrakutars continued their attack and conquered Kanauj and the fort of Kalanjara, circa AD940; once again it was the Chandella Yasovaram who upheld the honour of the Prathiharas. It was during the reign of the Rastrakutars that the magnificent rock-cut temples of Kailash at Ellora, and the huge carved halls at Elephanta Island near Bombay were constructed.

S

Surasundari *Surasundari* or celestial beauty, is a term used to describe the female figures that adorn the temples at Khajuraho and other temples. The Surasundari as conceived by the artist is elegantly proportioned, in the full bloom of womanhood and dressed in the fashions of the day.

T

Tri 'Tri' denotes three and is used in *trisul* or trident, and *trimurti* or image-with-three-faces. Siva is depicted carrying his trident or three-pronged spear with which he defeats his enemies. The sculptures at Khajuraho are rarely shown in static, or straight postures, the figures are in movement, standing in a relaxed pose with the knee of one leg bent, at ease. The posture called *tribhanga* refers to the three bends given to the body in the position of a dance pose.

V

Vatsa Vatsa is the ancient name of the region of Khajuraho that appears in inscriptions and literature. In the medieval period the region was called Jejabhukti and, after the fourteenth century, Bundelkand.

Vahana Vahana, the mount of Hindu gods and goddess, also represents some attributes of the gods. Siva rides Nandi the bull, symbolising strength and loyalty. Vishnu rides on Garuda, the mythical eagle, Brahma on a *hansa* or swan and Parvati on a lion who leads her into battle and victory.

Y

Yoni Yoni is the symbol of the female sexual organ, represented in medieval art as the base or pedestal of the *linga* (phallic) image of Siva. The combination of the *yoni* and *linga* acquired a symbolic form in these objects of worship and denote the principles of life and creation, power and sustaining energy.

INDEX